Introduction

The VMG Edge is proud to present the 90 day challenge.

Through this 90 period we will guide you from beginning to end on how we can get your success of the FAST TRACK.

Most of all entrepreneur's that have obtained tremendous success mention that it started with their first 90 days in their business or lifestyle change.

THE VMG EDGE IS HERE TO HELP YOU WITH THAT!

This book is a step by step guide to help you go through day's 1-90!

We will cover all the major key actions needed in order for you to even start with this 90 day change!

- Your Mentality

- Creativity

- Ambition

- You're personal WHY?

- What action is needed?

First let's start it off by Mentally preparing you to even get started there's a certain state of mind you have to be in, In order for you to be able to complete this 90 day cycle!

Here's are the KEY points in which your mind has to go through in order for you to accomplish the task at hand.

- Your thoughts determine what you do and how you take action with your life.

- Control what you think about and your subconscious mind will manifest and create the opportunities and bring those people necessary to help you get to your goals faster.

- Take action to your thoughts and work to place the right events and situations so that the odds are in your favor.

- KEEP IT POSITIVE! - Negative thoughts lead to negative bank accounts!

- Have an attitude of gratitude, and you will go far!

- Write down everything that you are TRULY GREATFULL FOR IN LIFE!

START IT OFF BY SAYING I AM SO HAPPY AND GREATFUL THAT……

_____
_____
_____
_____
_____
_____
_____
_____

Now we have come to Creativity...

"Creativity is intelligence having fun"

Key points to remember about being creative and to help you go through your 90 days.

- Sir Isaac Newton didn't go to school for two years and in that time he discovered Newton's laws of Physics and The Law of Gravity.

- Be yourself and people will notice act like everyone else and you'll go unseen by all.
- Spend an hour getting to know yourself.
- Don't be afraid of GREATNESS.

Ambition is the unwilling faith of moving forward!

Don't let others failure determine your Success.

- If you have goals in mind just go after them don't let others tell you NO!
- Grab life by the balls and don't let anyone tell you otherwise.
- Have a NO FUCKS GIVEN drive towards your goals do whatever it take to accomplish them!

WRITE DOWN ALL THE THINGS THAT MOTIVATE YOU TO KEEP DRIVING FORWARD!

_____

_____

_____

_____

_____

_____

      _____

Through this book you will clearly see I could give 3 S**** less about what you have done in the past if you stuck with one thing so far , By now you would have gotten what you want most in life but you didn't so it's time to MIX IT UP!

Your WHY?

Why are you reading this book?

Why haven't you gotten better at everything you're doing?

Why are you getting your butt chewed out at work?

Why are you feeling down about where you are?

Why haven't you gotten RICH yet?

Why you are so broke!?

Why hasn't anything worked out for YOU?

Why is everyone doing better than ME?

YOU ARE THE REASON EVERYTHING YOU'RE GOING THROUGH IS NOT WORKING OUT CHANGE THAT SHIT!

IN MY LAST BOOK THE VMG EDGE GUIDE TO RELATIONSHIP MARKETING I SHOW YOU HOW TO GET THE REAL REASON WHY??

What ACTION is needed from you?

- Stop saying what you're going to do and just get it done already we are all tired of you saying I'm going to do this or that……ECT……
- Stop tip toeing around through life and start stomping the crap out of it strut your stuff!
- Stop procrastinating and take ACTION come on this is why we're here to make plays!
- Start acting like a COACH instead of a Player.

- VISION without Action is DAY-Dreaming

Make note of all the ACTIONS you're going to take!

_____

_____

_____

_____

_____

_____

_____

_____

_____

Now that we got all the PRE-Requisites done for the 90 days let's get into it!

I first started to use the 90 challenge when I was going from the Fitness industry over to the Major leagues of CAR Sales.

The following are guidelines to the 90 days and nothing should be changed in this process. To this day I life my life in 90 sprints to goals that I still have yet to achieve and you should do the same until you get to where you want to be!

By following this 90 day system on a daily basis you will see the smallest things in life seem HUGE!

I went from $7.25 an hour to Salary in just 90 days and you can do the same!

THE DAILY SCHEDULE TO THE 90 DAY CHALLENGE!

START IF OFF BY ANNOUNCING YOUR 90 DAY RULE ON ALL YOUR SOCIAL SITES LIKE FACEBOOK,TWITTER,YOUTUBE

SO OTHERS CAN SEE YOUR POSITIVE CHANGE HAPPENING WHILE THEY GET LEFT BEHIND!

Morning

-
- (I woke my butt up at 6 am every damn day)
- Remember your reason WHY? And write it down on an index card.
- Read it several times a day.
- If you haven't got your WHY? I want you to write it down.

_____

_____

_____

_____

_____

_____

_____

_____

_____

_____

_____

_____

Refer to my last book on how to find out WHY?

Once you do that every Morning from now on, so picture your WHY?

NEXT is Picture your life

This one is easy…Write down where you want to be in the Future down to the smallest detail.

_____

_____

_____

_____

_____

_____

_____

_____

_____

_____

Remember to be grateful!

Always remember someone out there has less in their life than you!

Last and final step of the day!

Read through everything that you have jotted down and don't forget to just relax there's no pressure for you success is not overnight it comes to those who work hard at it.

Get a calendar and start your 90 days today.

I'll see you on the other side.

NOTES:_____

_____

_____

_____

_____

_____

_____

_____

_____

_____

_____

_____

_____

_____

_____

_____

_____

_____

—

```
I am so happy and grateful for
:_____
_____
_____
_____
_____
_____
_____
_____
_____.
```

Index card cutouts.

YOUR WHY?

```
MY WHY?
:_____
_____
_____
_____
_____
_____
_____
_____
_____
_____.
```

WHAT ARE MY DREAMS?

WHERE DO I SEE MY SELF ?

:_____
_____
_____
_____
_____
_____
_____
_____
_____
_____.

VMG MARKETING FIRM LLC

VICTOR M. GALLARDO

www.vmgmarketingfirm.com

www.ingramcontent.com/pod-product-compliance
Lightning Source LLC
Chambersburg PA
CBHW081757170526
45167CB00009B/4055